The SEO Handbook for Non-Technical Professionals

By: Roggie Clark

Copyright

Title: The SEO Handbook for Non-Technical Professionals
Author: Roggie Clark

Published by Kindle Direct Publishing
410 Terry Ave N
Seattle, Washington, 98109
United States
https://kdp.amazon.com/en_US

Cover Design: Roggie Clark
Editing: Renee' Clark

Printed in the United States of America

Disclaimer

The views and opinions expressed in this book are those of the author and do not necessarily reflect the official policy or position of any individual, company, or organization cited or referenced in the text.

The author is not affiliated with any of the individuals, companies, or organizations mentioned in the text, nor does the author receive any form of compensation for citing or referencing them. Some sample scenarios in this text are fictitious. Any similarity to actual persons, living or dead, is coincidental.

The professional information (strategies, tips, and concepts) in this text is distributed on an "as is" basis, without warranty. While every precaution has been taken in the preparation of the text to ensure all information is accurate, neither the author nor the publisher shall have any liability to any person or entity with respect to any loss or damage caused or alleged to be caused directly or indirectly by the instructions contained in this text or by the computer software and hardware products described in it.

Neither the author nor the publisher guarantees any specific results or outcomes, and the information provided in this text should not be construed as professional advice. Readers should always consult with a qualified professional before making any significant changes to their website or business.

By reading this text, you agree that the author nor the publisher is responsible for any direct, indirect, incidental, or consequential damages that may arise from the use of the information provided. You assume full responsibility for any actions taken based on the information presented in this text.

Table of Contents

Introduction

Search engine optimization plays a quiet but important role in how information, businesses, and ideas are discovered online. Even for professionals who do not write code or manage websites, SEO often influences visibility, traffic, and credibility in ways that are not always obvious. Marketing campaigns, content strategies, and business decisions are frequently affected by how search engines interpret and present information.

Many non-technical professionals interact with SEO indirectly. Writers may be asked to "optimize" content without fully understanding what that means. Managers may review SEO reports filled with unfamiliar terms. Business owners may invest in SEO services without a clear picture of what success should realistically look like. This disconnect often leads to confusion, misplaced expectations, and unnecessary frustration.

This book was written to provide clarity without requiring technical expertise. It explains how SEO works using plain language and practical examples, focusing on understanding rather than execution. Instead of teaching coding skills or advanced configurations, it helps readers understand how search engines evaluate content, how websites are discovered, and how SEO fits into broader marketing and business goals.

Understanding SEO does not mean becoming an SEO specialist. For non-technical professionals, the goal is awareness and context. When you understand the basic principles behind search visibility, you are better equipped to ask informed questions, evaluate advice, and make decisions that align with long-term objectives. You can collaborate more effectively with developers and SEO teams without needing to speak in technical terms.

SEO is often misunderstood as a collection of tricks or shortcuts designed to manipulate rankings. In reality, it is a discipline focused on relevance, clarity, and usefulness. Search engines aim to connect people with information that best meets their needs. When SEO is approached thoughtfully, it supports content quality, user experience, and sustainable growth.

This book is designed to be read at your own pace. Each chapter builds understanding step by step, without assuming prior knowledge. Whether you are a marketer, writer, manager, student, or business professional, the goal is to help you think clearly about SEO and understand how it influences the work you already do.

By the end of this book, you will not be expected to implement technical changes or master complex tools. Instead, you will have a solid foundation for understanding SEO, communicating confidently with specialists, and making informed decisions without confusion or guesswork.

Chapter 1: What SEO Is and What It Is Not

Search engine optimization is often discussed as if it were a shortcut to online success, but for non-technical professionals, this framing can be misleading. SEO plays a supporting role in how information is discovered and presented online, and understanding its true purpose helps set realistic expectations. This chapter establishes a clear foundation by explaining what SEO is designed to do and, just as importantly, what it cannot do.

The Purpose of Search Engine Optimization

The primary purpose of SEO is to help search engines understand content and determine when it is relevant to a user's search. SEO focuses on clarity, organization, and usefulness rather than manipulation. When content is structured and presented in a way search engines can interpret easily, it becomes more likely to appear in appropriate search results.

SEO supports discoverability. It helps ensure that valuable information is not overlooked simply because it is unclear or poorly presented. For non-technical professionals, this means SEO acts as a bridge between content creation, user needs, and search engine interpretation.

Common Misunderstandings About SEO

A common misunderstanding is that SEO is a guaranteed path to rankings or traffic. In reality, SEO improves opportunity, not certainty. Search engines weigh many factors when deciding what to display, and no amount of optimization can override competition or lack of demand.

Another misunderstanding is that SEO is primarily technical. While technical elements matter, many SEO decisions are shaped by content quality, messaging, and user intent. Non-technical roles influence SEO outcomes more than they often realize.

SEO vs Paid Advertising and Other Marketing Channels

SEO is frequently compared to paid advertising, but the two serve different purposes. Paid advertising delivers immediate visibility in exchange for budget. SEO builds visibility gradually by earning relevance and trust over time.

Unlike social media or paid campaigns, SEO does not depend on constant spending to maintain presence. However, it also does not offer instant results. Understanding these differences helps non-technical professionals evaluate where SEO fits within a broader marketing strategy.

Why SEO Is a Long-Term Discipline

SEO operates over extended timeframes. Search engines observe consistency, patterns, and ongoing relevance rather than isolated actions. Changes made today may take weeks or months to show measurable impact.

Because of this, SEO rewards patience and alignment rather than urgency. Long-term thinking allows SEO to support sustainable visibility, reduce reliance on paid channels, and strengthen overall digital presence.

Last Thoughts

Understanding what SEO is and what it is not provides a stable foundation for working with search visibility confidently. When SEO is viewed as a long-term discipline focused on clarity and relevance, it becomes easier to set realistic goals and evaluate progress. With this perspective in place, non-technical professionals can engage in SEO conversations with greater confidence and clarity.

Chapter 2: How Search Engines Understand Websites

Search engines are often described as complex or mysterious systems, which can make SEO feel intimidating to non-technical professionals. While the technology behind search engines is advanced, the basic process they follow is easier to understand than many people realize. This chapter explains how search engines find, interpret, and organize websites using simple concepts that do not require technical knowledge.

How Search Engines Discover Web Pages

Search engines discover web pages by following links. When a page is linked from another page that a search engine already knows about, it becomes easier to find. This process happens continuously as search engines move through the web, looking for new or updated content.

For non-technical professionals, this means that content does not exist in isolation. Pages that are not linked clearly within a website, or not referenced elsewhere online, may be difficult for search engines to discover. Discoverability is the first step before any ranking or visibility can occur.

How Pages Are Interpreted and Indexed

Once a search engine discovers a page, it attempts to understand what the page is about. It looks at the words used, how the information is organized, and how the page relates to other content. This information is then stored in a large database known as an index.

Indexing allows search engines to quickly retrieve relevant pages when someone performs a search. If a page is unclear, repetitive, or poorly organized, it becomes harder for search engines to categorize it accurately. Clear communication and structure help search engines interpret content more effectively.

Relevance, Authority, and Trust Explained Simply

Search engines rely on a few core concepts when deciding which pages to show. Relevance refers to how closely a page matches a search query. Authority reflects how established or credible a source appears based on signals such as links and consistency. Trust relates to reliability, accuracy, and overall user experience.

These concepts work together rather than independently. A page may be relevant but lack authority, or authoritative but not relevant to a specific search. Understanding this balance helps non-technical professionals see why good content alone is sometimes not enough for visibility.

Why Not All Pages Appear in Search Results

Not every page on a website is guaranteed to appear in search results. Some pages may not be discovered, others may not be indexed, and some may simply not be competitive enough to rank well. This does not always indicate a problem, but it does highlight the limits of search visibility.

Search engines aim to present the most useful results, not every possible result. Pages that lack clarity, relevance, or value may exist online without ever gaining meaningful exposure through search.

Last Thoughts

Understanding how search engines discover and interpret websites removes much of the mystery surrounding SEO. While the technology behind search engines is complex, the principles guiding visibility are rooted in clarity, relevance, and trust.

With this foundational understanding, non-technical professionals can better evaluate SEO decisions and understand how their work influences search visibility. In the next chapter, we will explore how content plays a central role in discoverability and relevance.

Chapter 3: Content, Relevance, and Discoverability

Content is at the center of how search engines connect users with information. For non-technical professionals, content is often the most familiar part of SEO, yet it is also one of the most misunderstood. This chapter explains how content supports search visibility by focusing on relevance, usefulness, and intent rather than optimization tricks.

What Makes Content Search Friendly

Search-friendly content is content that clearly communicates its purpose. It addresses a specific topic, uses language that reflects how people naturally search, and presents information in a structured and readable way. Search engines rely on these signals to understand what a page offers.

Clarity matters more than complexity. Content that is straightforward and well-organized is easier for both users and search engines to interpret. Search-friendly content focuses on answering real questions rather than forcing keywords into every sentence.

Quality vs Quantity in SEO Content

A common misconception is that producing more content automatically leads to better SEO results. While consistency matters, volume alone does not create relevance. Content that lacks purpose or originality often adds little value to search visibility.

High-quality content tends to perform better over time because it remains useful and accurate. Fewer well-developed pages often outperform large volumes of thin or repetitive content. For non-technical professionals, prioritizing usefulness over output helps support sustainable SEO efforts.

How Search Intent Shapes Content

Search intent refers to the reason behind a search. People may be looking for information, comparing options, or preparing to take action. Understanding intent helps shape content that matches what users actually want.

When content aligns with intent, it feels natural rather than forced. Search engines favor pages that meet user expectations, which is why understanding intent is more important than targeting specific keywords alone.

Why Useful Content Outperforms Optimized Content

Content designed solely for search engines often fails to engage real readers. Over-optimized content can feel unnatural, repetitive, or shallow. Search engines increasingly prioritize usefulness because it leads to better user experiences.

Useful content answers questions clearly, provides context, and respects the reader's time. When content genuinely helps users, it naturally aligns with search engine goals, making optimization less about manipulation and more about communication.

Last Thoughts

Content drives SEO by serving as the primary connection between user needs and search engine interpretation. When content is created with clarity, relevance, and intent in mind, it supports discoverability without relying on technical complexity.

Understanding this relationship allows non-technical professionals to contribute meaningfully to SEO efforts through thoughtful content decisions. In the next chapter, we will explore how website structure supports content visibility without requiring coding knowledge.

Chapter 4: Website Structure Explained Without Code

Website structure plays a quiet but important role in how search engines and users navigate information. For non-technical professionals, structure can feel abstract because it exists behind the scenes. This chapter explains how websites are organized and why structure matters, without requiring any coding knowledge.

How Websites Are Organized Behind the Scenes

Websites are made up of individual pages that are connected through navigation and links. These connections help both users and search engines move from one piece of information to another. A well-organized website groups related content together in a logical way.

From a non-technical perspective, structure is about hierarchy. Main topics are supported by related subtopics, and important pages are easier to reach. When information is organized clearly, search engines can better understand the purpose and relationships between pages.

Pages, Navigation, and Internal Linking

Navigation menus and internal links guide visitors through a website. They also signal importance to search engines by showing which pages are central and how content is connected. Pages that are linked clearly are easier to find and understand.

Internal linking helps distribute attention across a website. When content is isolated or poorly linked, it may be overlooked by search engines. Non-technical professionals influence this process through content planning and site organization decisions.

Why Structure Impacts Visibility

Structure affects visibility because it influences discoverability and context. Pages that are buried deep within a site or disconnected from related content are harder for search engines to prioritize. Clear structure helps search engines recognize which pages matter most.

A logical structure also improves user experience. When visitors can find what they need easily, they are more likely to stay engaged. Search engines take these behavioral signals into account when evaluating websites.

Common Structural Issues Non-Technical Teams Face

Non-technical teams often encounter structural issues without realizing it. These include duplicate content, unclear page purpose, or inconsistent navigation. These problems can dilute visibility even when the content itself is strong.

Misalignment between content strategy and website organization is another common challenge. When structure does not reflect how audiences think or search, SEO effectiveness suffers. Awareness of these issues helps teams collaborate more effectively with technical specialists.

Last Thoughts

Website structure supports SEO by providing clarity and context for both users and search engines. When structure is logical and aligned with content goals, visibility improves naturally. Non-technical professionals play an important role in shaping structure through planning and organization, even without direct technical involvement. In the next chapter, we will explore how keywords and search behavior connect SEO to real human intent.

Chapter 5: Keywords, Search Intent, and Human Behavior

Keywords are often the first concept people associate with SEO, yet they are frequently misunderstood. For non-technical professionals, keywords can seem like isolated phrases rather than signals of real human behavior. This chapter explains how keywords connect to intent, context, and the way people search, without reducing SEO to word matching.

What Keywords Represent

Keywords represent the language people use when searching for information. They reflect questions, needs, comparisons, and problems users are trying to solve. Keywords are not just terms to be inserted into content, but indicators of what people are thinking at a given moment.

Understanding keywords means understanding audience language. When content reflects how people naturally express their needs, it becomes easier for search engines to match that content with relevant searches.

How People Search and Why It Matters

People search in many different ways depending on urgency, familiarity, and intent. Some searches are short and broad, while others are detailed and specific. These differences influence what type of content best serves a query.

For non-technical professionals, recognizing these patterns helps shape messaging and content planning. SEO works best when it mirrors how people actually search, rather than forcing artificial language into content.

Search Intent Types Explained

Search intent generally falls into a few broad categories, such as informational, navigational, or action oriented. Informational searches seek answers or understanding. Navigational searches aim to find a specific site or resource. Action oriented searches suggest readiness to make a decision or take a step.

Content that aligns with intent feels relevant and useful. When intent is ignored, even well-written content may struggle to gain visibility because it does not meet user expectations.

Moving Beyond Exact Match Thinking

Exact match thinking focuses on placing specific keywords into content as often as possible. This approach is outdated and often counterproductive. Search engines are designed to understand meaning, context, and related concepts.

Moving beyond exact match thinking allows content to be written naturally. When content addresses topics thoroughly and clearly, it supports a wider range of searches without relying on repetition or rigid phrasing.

Last Thoughts

Keywords serve as a bridge between human behavior and search engine interpretation. When keywords are understood as signals of intent rather than targets to manipulate, SEO becomes more intuitive and effective. For non-technical professionals, this perspective supports better content decisions and more meaningful collaboration with SEO teams. In the next chapter, we will examine how SEO fits into broader marketing and business strategy.

Chapter 6: How SEO Fits Into Marketing and Business Strategy

SEO is most effective when it supports broader marketing and business goals rather than operating in isolation. For non-technical professionals, understanding where SEO fits within strategy helps prevent misalignment and unrealistic expectations. This chapter explains how SEO works alongside other efforts to support long-term growth.

SEO as a Supporting Channel, Not a Standalone Solution

SEO works best when it complements other marketing channels. It supports visibility, reinforces messaging, and helps sustain discoverability over time. SEO alone cannot carry an entire marketing strategy or compensate for weak fundamentals.

When SEO is treated as a standalone solution, it often becomes disconnected from real business needs. Integrating SEO with content, branding, and outreach allows it to function as part of a cohesive strategy.

Aligning SEO With Business Goals

SEO efforts should reflect clear business objectives. Whether the goal is awareness, education, or customer acquisition, SEO should support outcomes that matter to the organization. Without alignment, SEO activity can produce traffic without meaningful impact.

For non-technical professionals, this alignment begins with understanding priorities. Clear goals help guide content focus, measurement, and resource allocation.

SEO and Brand Building

SEO and branding are closely connected. Search visibility reinforces brand recognition by placing consistent messaging in front of audiences over time. When content reflects brand values and expertise, SEO helps build familiarity and trust.

Strong brands often perform well in search because they provide clear signals of authority and relevance. SEO supports brand building by amplifying consistency rather than replacing branding efforts.

Where SEO Fits in the Customer Journey

SEO interacts with multiple stages of the customer journey. It helps introduce people to information, guide research, and support decision-making. Different types of content serve different stages of this process.

Understanding where SEO fits allows teams to create content that supports users throughout their journey. This perspective prevents overemphasis on immediate outcomes and encourages long-term engagement.

Last Thoughts

SEO becomes more effective when it is viewed as a strategic support system rather than a standalone tactic. By aligning SEO with business goals, branding, and the customer journey, non-technical professionals can help ensure that search visibility contributes to meaningful outcomes. In the next chapter, we will explore how to work effectively with developers and SEO specialists.

Chapter 7: Working Effectively With Developers and SEO Specialists

SEO often requires collaboration between technical and non-technical teams. When communication breaks down, projects stall or produce disappointing results. This chapter focuses on how non-technical professionals can work productively with developers and SEO specialists without needing to understand technical details.

Understanding Roles and Responsibilities

Developers, SEO specialists, and non-technical professionals each play distinct roles. Developers focus on implementation and technical stability. SEO specialists analyze performance and provide guidance. Non-technical professionals shape messaging, priorities, and business context.

Clear role definition helps prevent overlap and confusion. When each group understands its responsibilities, collaboration becomes more efficient and outcomes improve.

How to Communicate Without Technical Language

Effective communication does not require technical vocabulary. Clear goals, examples, and context are often more useful than jargon. Non-technical professionals can describe desired outcomes rather than specific implementations.

Asking questions about impact and tradeoffs helps align efforts. Open communication creates shared understanding without requiring technical expertise.

Setting Expectations and Timelines

SEO improvements often take time to show results. Setting realistic expectations around timelines helps prevent frustration and misinterpretation. Clear milestones and check-ins support transparency.

Understanding that SEO involves testing and adjustment allows teams to remain flexible. Patience and consistency contribute to stronger long-term outcomes.

Avoiding Misalignment and Friction

Misalignment often arises from unclear goals or unrealistic assumptions. When expectations are not shared, teams may work toward different outcomes. Regular communication helps identify issues early.

Respecting each team’s expertise reduces friction. Collaboration improves when non-technical professionals focus on strategy and context while trusting specialists to handle execution.

Last Thoughts

Successful SEO collaboration depends on clarity, communication, and mutual understanding. Non-technical professionals play an important role by providing direction and context rather than technical instructions. When teams work together effectively, SEO efforts become more aligned, efficient, and impactful. In the next chapter, we will explore how to understand SEO reports and performance metrics.

Chapter 8: Understanding SEO Reports, Metrics, and Performance

SEO reports often feel overwhelming to non-technical professionals. They can include unfamiliar metrics, charts, and terminology that make it difficult to determine what actually matters. This chapter explains how to read SEO reports with clarity and focus, without getting lost in technical details.

Common SEO Metrics Explained

SEO reports often include metrics such as impressions, clicks, rankings, and traffic. Impressions are how many times the content has been seen, clicks is how many times it's been clicked on, rankings is where on the search results the content generally appears (1st, 2nd, 3rd, etc.), and traffic is just a general way to describe the amount of actual visitors the website has, like who actually stayed and clicked on stuff on your website.

Overall, these numbers indicate how content is performing in search results and how users interact with it. Each metric provides context rather than a complete picture on its own.

Understanding the purpose of each metric helps prevent misinterpretation. No single number defines success, and changes should be evaluated over time rather than in isolation.

What Reports Can and Cannot Tell You

SEO reports show patterns and trends, not guarantees or explanations. They can indicate progress, stagnation, or decline, but they do not always explain why changes occur. External factors such as competition and seasonality also influence performance.

Reports are most useful when combined with context. Non-technical professionals can use them to ask informed questions rather than draw immediate conclusions.

Measuring Progress Without Obsessing Over Rankings

Rankings receive a lot of attention, but they are only one indicator of performance. Visibility, engagement, and relevance often provide a more accurate picture of SEO impact. Rankings can fluctuate without reflecting meaningful change.

Focusing on broader trends helps maintain perspective. Progress in SEO is usually gradual and measured over extended periods.

Using Data to Support Decisions

SEO data should inform decisions rather than drive reactionary changes. Patterns over time help identify what is working and where adjustments may be needed. Data is most valuable when it supports strategic goals.

Non-technical professionals can use data to guide planning, prioritize efforts, and evaluate advice. Understanding the story behind the numbers leads to better decision-making.

Last Thoughts

SEO reports become more useful when they are viewed as tools for understanding rather than judgment. By focusing on trends, context, and alignment with goals, non-technical professionals can interpret performance with confidence. In the next chapter, we will address common SEO myths that often cause confusion and misaligned expectations.

Chapter 9: Common SEO Myths That Confuse Non-Technical Teams

SEO is surrounded by myths that often lead to unrealistic expectations and poor decision-making. For non-technical professionals, these misconceptions can make SEO seem either far more powerful or far less useful than it really is. This chapter addresses some of the most common SEO myths and explains why they continue to cause confusion.

SEO Is a One-Time Task

One of the most persistent myths is that SEO can be completed once and then left alone. This belief usually comes from viewing SEO as a checklist rather than an ongoing process. In reality, search environments, competitors, and user behavior constantly change.

SEO requires maintenance and adjustment over time. Content needs updating, structure may need refinement, and performance must be reviewed regularly. Treating SEO as a one-time task often leads to declining results and missed opportunities.

SEO Guarantees Rankings or Traffic

Another common myth is that SEO guarantees specific rankings or traffic levels. Search engines do not offer guarantees, and no one can control search results completely. SEO improves the likelihood of visibility, but outcomes depend on many factors beyond direct control.

Believing in guarantees often leads to disappointment or misplaced blame. Understanding uncertainty helps teams set realistic goals and evaluate performance more fairly.

More Content Automatically Means Better Results

Producing large amounts of content is sometimes mistaken for an SEO strategy. While consistency matters, quantity alone does not create relevance or authority. Content without purpose or differentiation often fails to perform well.

Search engines prioritize usefulness and clarity. Fewer high-quality pages often outperform large volumes of thin or repetitive content. Strategic content creation produces better long-term results than volume-driven approaches.

Tools Can Replace Strategy

SEO tools are helpful, but they do not replace thinking or planning. Tools provide data, suggestions, and diagnostics, but they cannot define goals or understand business context. Relying solely on tools often leads to mechanical decisions.

Strategy provides direction. Tools support execution. Non-technical professionals play a key role in shaping strategy by aligning SEO efforts with real objectives.

Last Thoughts

SEO myths persist because they offer simple answers to complex problems. By recognizing and moving beyond these misconceptions, non-technical professionals can engage with SEO more realistically and productively. Clear understanding helps set better expectations, improve collaboration, and support sustainable results. In the next chapter, we will explore what SEO can realistically achieve and where its limitations lie.

Chapter 10: What SEO Can Realistically Achieve and What It Cannot

SEO is often discussed in extremes, either as a powerful solution to every visibility problem or as an ineffective effort that fails to deliver results. For non-technical professionals, understanding the realistic capabilities and limits of SEO is essential for making informed decisions. This chapter clarifies what SEO can help accomplish and where its influence ends.

Problems SEO Can Help Solve

SEO can improve discoverability by making content easier for search engines to find and understand. It helps connect relevant information with users who are actively searching for it. When aligned with real demand, SEO supports steady, organic visibility.

SEO also helps reinforce credibility by positioning useful content consistently in search results. Over time, this visibility can strengthen brand recognition and support trust with audiences who repeatedly encounter the same source.

Problems SEO Cannot Fix

SEO cannot fix fundamental business problems. It cannot make a poor product appealing, replace customer service, or compensate for unclear messaging. Visibility alone does not create value if the underlying offering fails to meet user needs.

SEO also cannot create demand where none exists. If people are not searching for a product or topic, optimization will not generate interest. Understanding this limitation prevents unrealistic expectations.

The Limits of Search Visibility

Search results are competitive by nature. Only a limited number of positions exist on each results page, and search engines choose what they believe best serves users. SEO increases opportunity, not entitlement.

External factors such as competition, seasonality, and algorithm changes influence visibility. These factors are outside direct control and must be considered when evaluating performance.

Why Expectations Matter

Unrealistic expectations often lead to frustration or misinterpretation of results. Clear expectations help teams measure progress appropriately and stay focused on long-term goals. SEO performs best when given time and patience.

For non-technical professionals, setting reasonable expectations allows SEO to support sustainable growth rather than short-term pressure.

Last Thoughts

Understanding what SEO can and cannot do provides clarity and balance. When SEO is viewed as a supporting discipline rather than a guaranteed solution, it becomes easier to evaluate its role and impact. With realistic expectations in place, non-technical professionals can make better decisions and build stronger, more sustainable SEO strategies. In the next chapter, we will focus on SEO decision-making for managers and business owners.

Chapter 11: SEO Decision-Making for Managers and Business Owners

Managers and business owners are often responsible for approving SEO budgets, evaluating advice, and making strategic decisions without being deeply involved in execution. For non-technical decision-makers, SEO can feel difficult to assess because results are indirect and timelines are long. This chapter focuses on how to make sound SEO decisions without needing technical expertise.

Evaluating SEO Proposals and Advice

SEO proposals often include promises, projections, or technical language that can be difficult to interpret. A strong proposal should clearly explain goals, scope, and expectations rather than guarantee outcomes. Transparency matters more than certainty.

Non-technical decision-makers should focus on reasoning rather than tactics. Understanding why an approach is recommended helps distinguish thoughtful strategy from generic advice.

Budgeting and Resource Considerations

SEO requires time, effort, and coordination across teams. Budgeting for SEO involves more than paying for tools or services. It includes content creation, collaboration, and ongoing maintenance.

Allocating resources realistically helps avoid underinvestment or misalignment. SEO tends to perform better when supported consistently rather than treated as a short-term expense.

Knowing When to Invest More and When Not To

Not every situation requires increased SEO investment. Sometimes the issue lies outside of search visibility, such as product fit or messaging clarity. Recognizing these scenarios helps prevent wasted effort.

Conversely, sustained progress may indicate that additional investment could amplify results. Decision-makers benefit from evaluating trends over time rather than reacting to short-term changes.

Making Informed SEO Tradeoffs

SEO decisions often involve tradeoffs between speed, scope, and sustainability. Faster results may require higher costs or risk, while slower approaches tend to build durability. Understanding these tradeoffs supports better planning.

Non-technical professionals can guide tradeoffs by prioritizing long-term value and alignment with business goals rather than immediate gains.

Last Thoughts

Effective SEO decision-making does not require technical mastery. It requires clarity, patience, and alignment with broader objectives. By focusing on reasoning, resources, and tradeoffs, managers and business owners can support SEO efforts that deliver meaningful value over time. In the next chapter, we will explore how to build long-term SEO awareness without becoming technical.

Chapter 12: Building Long-Term SEO Awareness Without Becoming Technical

SEO changes over time, but the underlying principles that guide it remain relatively stable. For non-technical professionals, the goal is not to chase trends or master tools, but to build lasting awareness that supports better decisions. This chapter focuses on how to maintain SEO understanding over time without becoming technical or overwhelmed.

Developing SEO Literacy Over Time

SEO literacy is the ability to understand how search visibility works at a conceptual level. It allows non-technical professionals to recognize sound advice, ask informed questions, and avoid common misconceptions. This literacy develops gradually through exposure and reflection rather than intensive study.

Reading reports, observing patterns, and staying engaged in discussions all contribute to SEO literacy. Over time, this awareness becomes part of how professionals evaluate content, strategy, and performance.

Staying Informed Without Chasing Trends

SEO trends often create urgency and confusion. While changes do occur, most do not require immediate action or deep technical involvement. Staying informed means understanding direction, not reacting to every update.

Reliable sources, thoughtful analysis, and long-term observation help filter meaningful changes from noise. Non-technical professionals benefit from focusing on principles rather than temporary tactics.

Creating a Sustainable SEO Mindset

A sustainable SEO mindset values consistency, clarity, and patience. It recognizes that meaningful visibility builds over time and reflects real user needs. This mindset reduces pressure and supports thoughtful planning.

When SEO is approached as an ongoing discipline rather than a series of fixes, it integrates naturally into everyday work. This perspective helps teams maintain momentum without burnout.

How to Use SEO Knowledge Moving Forward

SEO knowledge becomes most valuable when applied thoughtfully. Non-technical professionals can use their understanding to guide strategy, evaluate recommendations, and support collaboration. This knowledge informs decisions without requiring direct implementation.

By maintaining awareness and perspective, SEO becomes a familiar part of professional judgment rather than an intimidating specialty.

Last Thoughts

Building long-term SEO awareness allows non-technical professionals to engage with search visibility confidently and realistically. Understanding principles, staying informed thoughtfully, and maintaining a sustainable mindset make SEO more approachable and effective. With this foundation, SEO becomes a tool for clarity and alignment rather than confusion, supporting better outcomes across marketing, content, and business decisions.

Conclusion: Thinking Clearly About SEO Moving Forward

Search engine optimization does not need to feel technical, mysterious, or overwhelming to be useful. For non-technical professionals, understanding SEO is less about execution and more about perspective. When SEO is viewed through the lens of clarity, relevance, and long-term thinking, it becomes easier to work with and evaluate.

Throughout this book, the focus has been on understanding how SEO functions within real-world contexts. Rather than emphasizing tools or tactics, the goal has been to explain how search engines interpret information, how content supports discoverability, and how SEO aligns with broader marketing and business objectives. This foundation allows professionals to engage with SEO confidently without needing technical expertise.

Clear understanding leads to better communication. When non-technical professionals understand SEO principles, conversations with developers, specialists, and agencies become more productive. Expectations are set more realistically, decisions are made more thoughtfully, and collaboration improves.

SEO is not a shortcut or a guarantee, but it is a valuable discipline when applied with patience and intention. It supports visibility, reinforces credibility, and helps useful information reach the people who are actively looking for it. When SEO is treated as a long-term effort rather than a quick fix, its impact becomes more meaningful and sustainable.

Moving forward, the most important takeaway is not mastery, but awareness. By maintaining a clear understanding of how SEO works and what it can realistically achieve, non-technical professionals can continue to make informed decisions and contribute to successful outcomes. SEO does not require you to become technical, it simply requires you to think clearly.

www.ingramcontent.com/pod-product-compliance
Lightning Source LLC
LaVergne TN
LVHW022324200926
848481LV00004B/1420
* 9 7 9 8 2 9 5 6 2 0 7 5 1 *